What You Didn't Learn in Teacher Training

From the Notebooks of Nelly Damon

Eugene Schwartz

ISBN 0-945803-36-2

Rudolf Steiner College Press
9200 Fair Oaks Blvd.
Fair Oaks, California 95628

Table of Contents

Editor's Disclaimer

Following the unexpected popularity of *The Waldorf Teacher's Survival Guide*, a number of readers asked me when Nelly would "have more to say," as she promised in the *Guide's* final conversation. As those who know her can attest, Nelly *always* has more to say, whether in word or print, and, for the last three years, she has been actively jotting down her random thoughts, and has decided to share them without further "polish." Nelly reasoned that a "finished" book, no matter how well-written, is invariably a *passive* experience for the reader. Everything has been thought out, worked out, and arranged to have a calculated effect on the book's audience. By sharing only her notes, Nelly draws us all into the creative process that would be hidden in a finished volume. We can pick and choose among them, discard those jottings which we don't need and let others, seed-like, germinate within us. This latter, *co-creative* experience is undoubtedly more amenable to the audience of inwardly-active Waldorf teachers for whom our book is intended.

Since the *Survival Guide's* appearance, "Nelly Damon" has been identified as the *nom de plume* of

Virginia Sease, Astrid Schmitt-Stegmann and Jane Wulsin, among others. When I protest such blatant untruths, speculation inevitably turns to the possibility that I am Nelly. Theories have been advanced that *I* suffer from Multiple Personality Disorder, or that I am so far along in developing my "Inner Child" that I have regained the etheric forces needed to create an Imaginary Friend. On a number of occasions I have been asked, "If Nelly Damon is so smart, then why hasn't she ever been invited to lecture at an AWSNA National Teachers' Conference?" In the interactive spirit in which this book has been written and edited, I will leave it to our readers to answer these questions for themselves.

A number of correspondents complained about the discursiveness of the first volume, and mentioned that they had to spend an inordinate amount of time searching for Nelly's comments on a particular matter. To help with this, I have arranged her remarks according to the subjects she covers, and a table of contents has been provided.*

Nelly has been pleased to share her insights with me, and I am delighted to share them with you. Like Nelly, I hope that you all view the present accomplishments of the Waldorf movement with pride, and look forward to our future challenges with justified optimism.

Eugene Schwartz
Spring Valley, NY
Advent, 1996

* Ms. Damon insisted that her unhappiness about this innovation be made known, "I object to this scholastic approach, which is better suited to the ivory towers of academia than to the realities of the Waldorf movment. Next thing you know Eugene will be inserting footnotes!"

Author's Protest

As if it were not intrusive enough for Eugene Schwartz to be forever following me about, tape recorder in hand, he has now decided to make my most personal jottings matters of public record. Even though he is well aware that I am opposed to hagiography in *any* form, Eugene insists on subtitling this book "From the Notebooks of Nelly Damon." That moniker, of course, says no more about the value of these contents than a designer label says about the quality of a pair of jeans. My protests to him have been of no avail. The man is incorrigible, and I am sure that he is already at work on a third volume whose title will be *Our Daily Bread: The Collected Shopping Lists of Nelly Damon.*

To convince me to part with my notebooks, Eugene reminded me that I had declared, at the conclusion of *The Waldorf Teacher's Survival Guide* "I have more to say." Indeed, I have entertained thoughts about a second book, and even considered such titles as *Survival Guide: The Sequel*, or *Son of Survival Guide* (California title: *Son/Daughter of Survival Guide*). Unfortunately, not all of us have the luxury, like Eugene, of taking a year off whenever we please (how does his school let him get away with that?). Between my own class preparation, countless (and endless) meetings and all of the ills that flesh is heir to, I have found it impossible to convert the handwritten raw material presented here into anything more than *typed* raw material.

The thoughts expressed herein are nothing but thoughts; they were only to jog my memory when the time came for me to write a *real* book about the challenges that continue to face the Waldorf Movement, and its teachers, at the Millennium's end. Notwithstanding Yeats' remarks about poetry, I am not pleased to have such "conversations with myself" formatted on someone's computer and presented as a finished piece of work. It was only Eugene's earnest entreaties that led me to believe that even a half-baked loaf might provide some nourishment for a select number of insight-hungry Waldorf teachers.

My apologies for the pretentious title that the editor has chosen. When he speaks of matters that "you didn't learn in Teacher Training," he doesn't necessarily imply that those matters weren't *taught* to you; it could very well be that, at the time, you didn't want to hear about them. Whether you will be any more inclined to heed some difficult advice just because it now appears in *print* is an open question.

These lines are being written as I sit on the Piazza San Marco in Venice, enveloped by autumnal sunlight and Adriatic breezes. The Basilica San Marco looks as if it were designed and built by a host of euphoric children who were told to make manifest their imagination of Heaven. The Lions of St. Mark are smiling, the four bronze horses that traveled from Constantinople to alight on the Basilica's roof are smiling, and the entire Piazza, with its countless people and ubiquitous pigeons, is making one great smile, a gesture of joy that embraces earth and heaven alike.

Why, I wonder, don't Waldorf teachers smile like that? Why are our younger teachers so stressed and uncertain, so ill-prepared and unsupported? Why are our older teachers so reluctant to take the lead, so loath to change their outdated ways, and so defensive about their utterly conventional methods? Why is there so little joy in an educational movement that should one day be the moral equivalent of a medieval cathedral or Renaissance basilica?

I can't say that the answer to any of those questions is to be found in the enclosed pastiche. However, in my next book . . .

Nelly Damon
Venice,
Michalemas, 1994

Working with Parents

Beware of intellectual snobbism in regard to parents. Example: "How can I talk to parents about the etheric body, the astral body, etc.? I've had such a hard time with those concepts in my training—surely *they* could never understand it!" For all that you know: 1) they may be much further along than you are in spiritual development, and 2) how are you ever going to clarify your own understanding of these matters unless you try to bring them into relation to your own experience and share them with others?

◆

What Parents Say:

My child is bored; give him more of a *challenge*!

What Parents Mean:

My son fears that he will fail when he is asked to do something new, such as knitting, or singing, or jumping rope. Couldn't you ask him to do only those things that come to him *easily* to him, such as reading and math problems?

◆

How can you "bond" with parents who come new to the class in a later grade—and how can the bonds with old parents be ceaselessly renewed? Begin each new school year with a "Parent's Intensive": a Saturday morning workshop held in September. Provide child care and *insist* that every family be represented if they want their child to remain in the class (yes, bonding with parents is a *serious* business!). A possible morning's schedule:

9:00	Parents introduce themselves
9:15	Teacher gives an imaginative and practical picture of the child at this particular grade level (not hesitating to talk about the "higher bodies," as well).
10:00	Refreshments and socializing
10:30	One or two "mini Main Lessons", to show the parents *how* you teach, and to give them a chance to see how challenging the work will be for their children.
12:00	Questions and discussion, or, for the really courageous, invite all the children in and share a story with them and their parents.
12:30	A pot-luck lunch

This should be followed up by a letter describing the morning and stating your appreciation for the parents' interest and support. We can never thank our parents often enough!

◆

Goals: The Waldorf curriculum can appear so esoteric and its practitioners can appear to be left so free in their interpretations of it, that parents often feel left in the dark concerning just what a teacher is going to accomplish in a given year—and when, and how. In late August, before the school year begins, send your parents: 1) A Main Lesson Block Schedule, 2) A narrative description of what will be taught in the coming year (and where possible, why), will be taught in the coming year, and 3) A month-by-month, or, better yet, week-by-week outline of exactly how you intend to unfold each subject.

By the year's end, do you expect that the children will be reading? Will they understand fractions in an introductory way only, or will they be able to find the least common denominator? How far along will they be in their grammar?

If this is your "first time through," spend part of your summer availing yourself of the experiences of a senior teacher who can help you establish realistic goals—but don't simply flounder around, or you'll join the (growing, alas) ranks of Waldorf teachers who desperately resort to public school textbooks and methods in the upper grades in order to make up for all of the time that they wasted in the early years.

◆

Parents can be highly sensitive to a "difficult" child's negative influence on their own child; but what about their child's positive effect on the malefactor? It is up to the teacher to see that first, and to help the parent see it as well.

◆

Social evenings with parents: From fifth grade on, class parents should form a "support group" to get them through the tumultuous years of their children's adolescence! One or two meetings a year should be held, not in the classroom, but rather in a home. Although the teacher can give some suggestions and guidance, she should year by year take a back seat, recognizing that matters such as curfews, party chaperones, and the type of movies suitable for sixth, seventh, and eighth graders must be agreed upon by the parents, for it is they who will take the final responsibility.

◆

Never forget that, when you are teaching, it is only one-third of the class who sits before you; the other two-thirds of the class are at work or at home. Keep the parents—the other two-thirds of your class—in your consciousness, for all that you impart in the way of education to the children will slowly, and often powerfully, educate the parents as well.

◆

A teacher never really asks a child to leave his class; it is the *parents* that we are telling to leave.

◆

In the early grades, parents want their child to be happy. In the later grades, parents want their child to be *successful*. Waldorf schools can meet both of these wishes, though neither is really our task. A child who is always happy will not be able to deepen what she has learned, and a child who is always successful will not encounter those mistakes and outright failures which are life's wisest teachers.

Perhaps we simply should drop the predicate nominatives and say that we want the child to learn to be.

◆

What Parents *Say*:

At some point you have to trust your child!

What Parents *Mean*:

I've given up trying to guide my 12-year-old daughter. I accept her judgment that although she is thirty years younger than I am and has virtually no life experience upon which to base her judgments, she is still capable of making far more intelligent decisions about her life than I can.

◆

You can ignore most of the praise that parents in your class lavish upon you, but take their criticisms to heart. When parents criticize you, you *know* that they are being sincere!

◆

Most of a Waldorf school's problems can be prevented at the "entry level." Teachers need to ask more probing questions, need to be more open about the school's philosophy and methodology, and need to assess families in a much more critical way *before* we accept them into our schools.

◆

A seminar on marriage counseling should be a requirement in all teacher training courses.

◆

Parents in the school: There must be an imaginary line at the school secretary/receptionist's desk or office beyond which no one ventures without permission. Why are Waldorf schools so often so casual about the sacred work going on within the classroom, letting parents drop off lunches, chat with their children, or come to fetch them at all times of day? Do families wander in and out of operating rooms while their loved ones are in surgery?

Do visitors to criminal trials accompany the lawyers when they confer with the judge in her chambers? If teachers don't take their work more seriously, why should the parents?

◆

As you go up the grades, even the most supportive parents in a younger grade begin to wonder whether the Waldorf curriculum, with its child-centered philosophy, its stress on the arts, its relatively light homework load etc., *really* will prepare their children for a mainstream junior high or high school. Shouldn't we begin getting the children ready for heavy homework loads, for examinations, for using textbooks?

My response: "As a conscientious parent, you are probably taking care that your child's diet is well-balanced, rich in natural foods, prepared with love etc. We know, of course, that once your child gets to college, he will probably have to eat a lot of relatively processed fare, including a good deal of junk food. Shouldn't you begin to prepare him *now* for that inevitable diet? Once or twice a week, serve junk food, gradually increasing the load until, by high school, you serve nothing *but* junk food . . ."

By now the parents are laughing. Obviously, the best way to prepare their child for his junk food diet is to nourish as well as possible in these formative years and to inculcate eating habits that will help him make intelligent choices later, in the "real world." And should we deal any differently with his education? Let us feed our students real *bread* as long as we can; the stones will come soon enough.

◆

When I meet with public school educators, they speak by the hour about the cultivation of *excellence*. Then I take out samples of Waldorf school main lesson books and say, "This is what we are doing to cultivate excellence." Their response is always the same. "Could you show us some of your *poorer* work?"

◆

Considering the types of problems that many Waldorf families experience today, which in turn impinge upon our work in the classroom, perhaps, along with *Discussions With Teachers* and *Study of Man* our teacher trainees should have *The National Enquirer* and *Rolling Stone* on their Required Reading list.

◆

Working with Colleagues

Following a tempestuous Board and Faculty meeting in an Hawaiian school, the notes and letters which constituted the basis of all the conflict were left out on the boardroom table. That night, I am told, one of the worst hurricanes in Hawaii's history struck the island, swept into the room, and carried the documents away.

◆

When a school on the East Coast faces a major administrative problem, the solution is ahrimanic: "Let's get better software!" When a West Coast school faces a similar problem, the solution is luciferic: "Let's have a sweat lodge!" When AWSNA faces the problem, the solution is eminently balanced: "Let's conduct a survey!"

◆

The special place held by the first grade and eighth grade class teachers: It is not the person, but the position. To paraphrase Goethe, we honor the eighth grade teacher because of all that he has been over the years, and the first grade teacher because of all that she may become. Yet year by year few schools appear to harbor high hopes for their present first grade teacher, and fewer still look back with affection and regard upon the achievements of their eighth grade teacher. If the foundation is weak and the pinnacle is crumbling, how can the center hope to hold?

◆

The state of near penury in which many Waldorf teachers find themselves leads them to solutions which seem to go in and out of style. The insurance salesman I mentioned in the *Survival Guide* is rapidly being replaced by the MLM (Multi-Level Marketing) sales representative. While the insurance salesman was usually somewhat crestfallen and embarrassed about his calling, the MLM rep is filled with enthusiasm for such endeavors as Amway and Shaklee (household cleansers and general merchandise) and Cell Tech (blue-green algae). Not only do teachers find a welcome source of extra income in such endeavors (in fact, for some the MLM commissions become their *primary* income); they also discover a setting in which hard work reaps financial benefits, and they become part of a group of coworkers who actually *praise one another* for their efforts.

The MLM connection thus provides what many a teacher once expected to find in the Waldorf school and did not; the satisfaction of providing a service that people are happy to use; remuneration which is commensurate with the amount of work that a person does; a supportive and lively group of colleagues who fervently believe in the service that they are offering. The hierarchical, "pyramidal" structure of the spiritual world with which teachers are supposed to find a connection in their College meetings is instead met in the MLM company's materialized structure.

Is it right for a person as influential as a Waldorf teacher to use her persuasive powers to sell detergents or food supplements? (Perhaps the same persuasive talents now used to sell soap and unicellular creatures could be used to "sell" Waldorf education to potential parents, raising the school's enrollment and guaranteeing pay raises for everyone!) How much effort can an already-overburdened class teacher put into Amway before she has that much less to give to her class? And, most importantly, will any of these questions ever be asked at a faculty meeting? Will the deeper question of what leads people to MLMs in the first place ever be addressed? (Don't hold your breath.)

◆

On the working together of class teachers and specialist teachers (a knotty problem in many Waldorf schools):

Just as a butterfly receives nourishment from individual flowers and only "inadvertently" pollinates and thus unites them, so the lower school child receives some particular gift from each of her teachers and "inadvertently" conveys it to every other teacher. The class teacher must recognize that every one of his students is reflecting not only what he has given, but also the essences of all of the specialist teachers.

This is also a good reason to have faculty meetings only on school days, when the children have been present to "cross-pollinate" us and bring us that much closer as colleagues.

◆

An autobiographical book by G. I. Gurdjieff was entitled *Meetings With Remarkable Men*. Were I to write the story of my travels amongst Waldorf schools, I might call it *Meetings With Unremarkable People*. As individuals, most Waldorf educators are rarely charismatic, sparkling or powerful; in many other school settings, they would not even make very good teachers. So what it is that allows such ordinary people to work in such an extraordinary way? I would contend that . . .[1]

1 This page in Nelly's notebook had suffered some water damage and the rest of the sentence was illegible. Nelly is herself unable to recall what she had written here.

Working with Students

Standards: the word has a military lineage, from the flag that was carried headlong into battle to direct soldiers. Most Waldorf teachers do not ask enough of their students. Recitations are sloppy, not practiced sufficiently or penetrated fully. In a class of twenty-five, only four or five of the "good artists" do true grade-level work, while the teacher accepts mediocre work from others. Christian "acceptance" of a child, warts and all, is valid on the level of soul; when transferred to the level of will, it saps children of any ambition to go beyond themselves. On the level of will, striving must predominate—the model provided by the teacher will guide the child, as once the banner of the "standard-bearer" guided armies to their goal.

◆

In the Lower School, the class teacher stands in the center, radiating the wisdom of the world to the children, who stand in a circle around him, like planets around the sun. In the High School, every student becomes a center who calls upon the diverse group of specialist teachers to form a circle around him.

◆

A good teacher inspires her students to show her their very best side at all times. A great teacher allows them to show her their worst side as well, or what is there for her to help the students transform?

◆

Heredity = Life/Bodily = Sleep

Individuality = Soul/Spiritual = Wakefulness

To mediate between the two, the Class Teacher must help the child learn to dream.

◆

It is good to teach the right content, but it is essential to teach it in the right context.

◆

The American school year begins twice. The first beginning comes at Michaelmas time, when school officially opens. The second comes after Easter (the time that some European schools officially open). This second beginning is already a foreshadowing of the school year to come.

◆

A school generally does well with its adolescent students until the school itself reaches its "adolescent phase," i.e. about fourteen years of age. It is hard enough to begin a High School even then, but unrealistic to create one before that point in the school's life.

◆

As a compromise, and to throw a sop to parents anxious to keep their children out of mainstream junior highs, a Waldorf school may consider extending the Lower School one more year and adding a ninth grade, with no intention to create a high school for some time to come.

But think about it—is the ninth grade, one of the most difficult and chaotic years in a human life, the one that you want your students to recall as their *last* year in your school? It is much better all around for the eighth grade to be recalled as the crowning year of their Waldorf school experience. The ninth grade is bearable only when there are three more years of Waldorf school still to come.

◆

If Alzheimer's Syndrome is the affliction of those who grew up in the 1930s (feebleness in thinking) and Chronic Depression is the affliction of "the Prozac Generation"—those who grew up in the 1960s—(weakness in feeling), then Hyperkineticism is the affliction of those growing up in the 90s (overwhelmed by willing). By helping our children to integrate the forces of thinking, feeling and willing we are not only healing them as individuals; we are taking a step towards the healing of our sick and weary century.

◆

What is the picture of world evolution that our culture gives to its children?

In the Beginning: *Jurassic Park*. A world filled with dinosaurs; savage and lush, overflowing with nature forces too powerful for human beings to bear.

In the End: *Star Trek*. A world created and sustained by technology; gleaming and sanitized, devoid of anything "natural," an artificial "planet" banded on all sides by a cosmic vacuum and inhabited as much by androids as by human beings.

Where can a child find her *humanity* between these luciferic and ahrimanic boundaries of time? Only through an education that bridges a *true* beginning and a *true* ending, that works with the One Who said, "I am the Alpha and the Omega . . ."

◆

One day parents will take their children through the Disneyworld of the future, and there, resplendent in plastic, will be life-like figures intently picking up sticks, creating dunes and caves in sandboxes and jumping rope.

"What are *those*, Mommy?"

"Oh those are *children*, dear. They are replicas of a now-extinct form of life that flourished for some time before the end of the 20th century."

◆

Will Waldorf education ever be at ease in our 30-second sound bite, bumper-sticker slogan society? So far, the prognosis isn't hopeful. Now that all of the bumper-stickers proclaiming *Waldorf: It's a School, Not a Salad!* have worn off the cars that bore them, another popular bumper sticker has appeared. *Its* sentence fragment says: Waldorf: Education from the Inside Out.

That sounds lovely, implying that Waldorf schools are sensitive to the child's inner life and filled with teachers undoubtedly "in touch with their feelings." But is it *true*? Do Waldorf schools educate from *within* and work their way *out*, pedagogically speaking?

Quite the contrary! In Kindergarten and the lower grades, the teacher takes the greatest pains to create an environment *around* the child so that the forms and colors, structures and habits with which the child is surrounded are gradually "breathed in" by the soul and ever so slowly help to mold the child's inner life.

To be true to ourselves, our bumper-sticker should say: *Education from the Outside In.* But that sounds superficial; perhaps it should be footnoted, to explain that what we mean by "outside" is not just skin-deep—a bibliography for further reading should be appended, and perhaps some samples of student work . . . On second thought, why don't we leave the bumper-sticker slogans to the rock music stations, after all?

◆

I visited a large and pricey stuffed animal store in Ithaca, and was told by the owner that virtually all of her customers are *students*, mostly from Cornell University. I was reminded of the experiences had by many Waldorf alumnae in their freshman dormitory rooms—*they* want to hang up modern art and have minimalist rooms, but their roommates, coming from mainstream schools that accelerated their intellectual development and forced them to skip their childhood, want stuffed toys and Disney posters. The Waldorf students experienced childhood when they were children, and are ready for a modern adulthood; their roommates may spend their lives searching for the childhood that was cut short.

◆

The seven-year milestones in a youngster's life are

not points of departure from which the child may take leaps into the next stage; they also offer opportunities for the child to experience something essential that he missed in the previous seven-year cycle.

For example, take a child who doesn't hear any fairy tales around the age of seven. His need for fairy tales appears to go away, but in reality it has merely withdrawn from consciousness, gone dormant, ready to return with a vengeance at about the next seven-year milestone, when the child reaches adolescence. Now it manifests as a need for fantasy, for escapist video games and comic books with their distorted fairy tale characters, or even as a craving to fully enter into the illusory world of drugs.

The Waldorf curriculum tries to give the child what she needs *when* she needs it, so that she can work through it and seek the next step in her life. Mainstream, overly-intellectualized education ignores developmental *needs* and so fosters *cravings* that fester in the soul.

◆

In Europe a far greater number of Waldorf schools are found in urban settings rather than in rural locations, but in the United States the opposite is true. American Waldorf school parents and teachers alike, despairing of the crime and squalor in urban areas, look for the most bucolic and beautiful natural settings in which to establish new schools, believing that a natural, relatively unspoiled environment will by itself have a beneficial effect on their children.

This certainly holds true for the first seven years of life, but as pubescence and adolescence approach, "Nature" no longer has the harmonizing and life-giving effect that it had in the child's earlier years. The most beautiful camping trip is shaken by the 12 year-old complaining nonstop of being bored. The beloved goats and horses and garden plots are neglected, or attended to with reluctance. Too often, the endless ennui the youngster claims to experience in this uneventful paradise can be mitigated only through the purchase of a VCR and huge stereo, so that a big dose of city life finds its way into the country at last. Indeed, by the time their children have reached this age, many parents sell their house in the country and move into town, recognizing that only the stimulation of friends and urban activities will keep their adolescents away from drugs and rural rutting. And, if nothing else, the parents have grown tired of being their child's non-stop chauffeur as she carries on long-distance friendships on endless country roads.

Once upon a time, "wholesome natural surroundings," all by themselves, were able to guarantee a relatively healthy and sound childhood and youth. Today I would contend that those surroundings can guarantee a healthy first six or seven years; nine years at best. *After* that age, the health and nourishment once given by Nature can today only be provided by *Culture*. *Too* many parents involved with rural Waldorf schools have rejected *everything* associated with urban or town life, including concerts and museums and the general "cultural ambiance" that can be experienced in a city. Especially west of the Rockies, many have turned their backs on the whole "Western mind-set" and thrown out the cultural baby with the sooty urban bathwater.

Nature without Culture has little to give the adolescent. To put it another way, the beneficial forces of Mother Nature are powerfully supportive of the child as a physical-etheric being, but have only a limited effect on the child as a physical-etheric-*astral* being. As the astral body approaches the child (age 9) and becomes incorporated in her own being (age 12-15) cultural forces are needed for support. Painting and drawing, singing and playing an orchestral instrument, conversation and poetry, become the stones and flowers, animals and clouds of the teenager's inner world. The more rural the setting, the more intensively the Waldorf school must raise its artistic standards, pursue a classical musical program, and encourage parents to cultivate a sense for artistic appreciation in their homes.

◆

My meeting with the poet Gary Snyder took place on the campus of a university in Colorado in the spring of 1969. Our discussion led me to share my thoughts of how external environmental problems resembled such physiological illnesses as clogging of the arteries (river pollution) or cancer (overcrowding, landfills). He was enthusiastic about these images, and then attributed all of the problems to the impact that overpopulation had on the environment.

"There are just too many goddamn children being born!" he declared.

"You're a Buddhist," I said, "And I suppose that you believe in reincarnation."

"Of course," Gary said.

"What if souls are *choosing* to reincarnate at this time? Don't you think that there is some *reason* that so many people want to be here on earth right now?"

Gary paused for a moment, then glared.

"Sure there's a reason!" he cried, "I'll tell you the reason! They're all a bunch of frigging *egomaniacs*!"

Now Rudolf Steiner explained this phenomenon in a somewhat different way . . .

We are very likely at the time of the greatest number of earthly incarnations in history. The spiritual world is "emptying out" as souls pour down, all of them wishing to be on the earth at this time of great spiritual crisis and challenge. It would stand to reason then (although "reason" doesn't always apply to anomalies of the spirit), that there are many now on the earth who would not ordinarily incarnate at the same time, who do not "share karma" in the usual sense. Might this explain a phenomenon that I have often observed that of learning-disabled children in a regular Waldorf class whose friends are all either much older or much younger than they are? Sometimes the greatest challenge—and the most effective "remediation"—for these youngsters is to get them to make friends with their classmates! Perhaps this problem sheds light on the question of "old" and "new" karma.

◆

Isn't it interesting that since the 60s young people have chosen to wear the jeans, the tee shirts, and the heavy boots that used to be worn only by *workmen*? Without knowing it, the generations that have incarnated in the last third of this century are acknowledging their connection to the domain of *willing*, rather than to the spheres of thinking and feeling so honored by their parents and teachers. Ironically, the youngsters who can afford these designer-enhanced workclothes (the more worn and deconstructed, the more costly they are) are the same youngsters who can hardly hammer a nail or walk more than a few hundred feet without fatiguing. Are their teachers helping them to unfold a will that is more than skin-deep, or are they merely paying lip-service to the Will in Waldorf education, providing only Designer Pedagogy—Waldorf Lite—instead of the Real Thing?

◆

Up until this century, the center of the home was the kitchen, and the center of the kitchen was the hearth—the fireplace or wood stove in which the warmth and radiant light of a flame expressed, to the open senses of the child, the warmth and glow of the familial life. Around this fire food was prepared and cooked, wash and bathwater was warmed, and gossiping neighbors, storytelling friends and Bible-reading grandparents gathered and lived their lives.

The hearth gave way to the gas stove, the gas stove to the electric range and the electric range to the microwave oven, each one, in turn, making the glowing flames less visible and the warmth of cooking less tangible.

And what is the center of today's kitchen? The refrigerator! Upon its sleek and impervious door we magnetically emblazon our family photographs, important phone numbers and appointments, and the credos by which we live. (How many a family involved with a young Waldorf school has attached to its refrigerator Goethe's verse beginning, "Whatever you can do, Or dream you can, Begin it . . . ?) The welcoming warmth of the hearth has been supplanted by the electronically controlled coldness of the refrigerator, which produces warmth only as an unwelcome byproduct. Food that is harvested, prepared and cooked is replaced by "meals" that are processed, that can be removed from the refrigerator by even the youngest child and "warmed' in a microwave–without the assistance or supervision of a busy adult.

Is the coldness so many children feel from their parents any mystery when we examine what has become of the "home and hearth?" Can we doubt our mandate as teachers to embody a "pedagogical hearth," one that radiates warmth and glows with enlightenment for our children?

◆

There ought to be a course on *Teaching Children How to Use the Bathroom.*

While the first grade teacher works contentedly with her well-behaved class, lulled into believing that everything is under control, little does she know what two little boys—allowed to use the bathroom at the same time—are doing in there! They are getting a hands-on course in hydraulics and pneumatics as they stuff wads of paper towelling into the toilet and watch it overflow, as they increase the pressure of the water tap by holding their fingers over the opening, as they soak crumpled-up balls of toilet paper with water and hurl them at the ceiling, where they remain, in defiance of the laws of gravity.

As much as I believe in the value of play as preparation for the understanding of the sciences at a later age, *supervised* play in the classroom or playground is preferable to havoc in the bathroom. Some suggestions:

- During class time the children should have a prearranged signal (such as the well-known "two fingers") by which they silently ask your permission to go out. They must wait for your silent nod before they leave. Children should not be free to come and go as they please.
- No more than one boy and/or one girl should use the bathroom at a time, unless you or another teacher are able to be near the bathroom yourselves.
- Every child who uses the bathroom should write her initials (or draw her symbol) on the

board when she leaves and erase it when she returns to the classroom.

Now and then the teacher should look into the bathroom and check its cleanliness and order and compliment the children if all is neat. Let them know that your consciousness extends into *all* areas.

Slowly but surely your students should develop increasing control over their bladders, which is an important foundation for the later mastery of their astral bodies. (When my seventh and eighth graders would besiege their language teachers with requests to use the bathroom, I would tell them that if they were able to sit through a 90-minute movie without leaving the theater, they were probably capable of sitting through a 50-minute French class). The more form and consciousness that a teacher brings to as mundane a matter as bathroom use, the more she is helping the class prepare for adolescence.

Working On Oneself

Family Values: Why, I am often asked, do Waldorf teachers have such unhappy families? Shouldn't we be setting the example of healthy family life for our school's parents? After all, we are always telling them to improve their family lives, to spend more time with their children, to cultivate a healthier rhythm etc. Aren't we being hypocritical? On the other hand, considering the time that a Waldorf teacher must spend simply preparing, and, in addition to that, the time that must be given over to faculty and College meetings, to committees, to the Christmas Fair, and to emergency conferences spent helping parents deal with *their* family crises, how is it possible to simply maintain, no less strengthen, one's own family life?

First of all, we must ask if it is true that Waldorf education in and of itself necessarily strengthens our school parents' family life. I can think of just as many families who have been divided or even split up by the conflicts caused by one parent's passionate commitment to the school. As soon as a parent begins to get as involved in the school as a teacher might be, her marriage begins to unravel! Why should this be happening, to teachers and parents alike, in a *Waldorf school* of all places?

The Archangel Gabriel has the task of supporting the family, but in our Michaelic Age—which is hardly a century old—Gabriel's support grows increasingly less effective, so that it takes more and more *human* will and effort to keep a family viable. In a Gabrielic age, family is responsible for education, as well as domestic life; in a Michaelic age, school grows increasingly responsible for domestic matters in addition to education! Michael's influence strengthens the relationship we cultivate with our co-workers, so that a new "family" feeling is created among those who work with a particular intensity, single-mindedness, or who keep work-hours that are out of synch with conventional rhythms (all of which apply to a Waldorf school setting).

Every Michael Age stresses the cosmopolitan and universally human over the insular and familial. (We need only think of Alexander the Great, torn between his father and mother in a classic "dysfunctional family" during the previous Michael Age, or the world-renowned breakdown of the Tolstoy family at the beginning of the present Michael Age, its dramatic finale played out in a railway station with newsreel cameras running.) In a Michael Age the arena of destiny relationships inevitably shifts from the family hearth to the workplace (or the battlefield). What we do in our work becomes more meaningful than what we do at home; the connections that we make with our co-workers becomes more interesting than the links that we have forged in our family.

Only insofar as workplace and family merge or coincide can the family in its present form be maintained (which may account for the growing number of "home offices" at the century's end).

As an engaging and intensely *interesting* place to work, the Waldorf school may very well stand as a bell-weather of changes that are sure to sweep the world in terms of family and vocation, heredity and individuality. Rather than bemoaning the breakdown of the family *as we know it* and demanding that Waldorf schools lead a retreat to older (Gabrielic) values, we must cultivate the courage to search for new "family values." These values would be founded on the mutual *interest that spouses develop in one another's vocation*, so that family life may be based on future-directed free ego-activity and not merely on the etheric and astral bonds of the past.

◆

We are meant to be knights, interacting with the world (a Michaelic attitude); not monks, withdrawing from it.

◆

How strange that teachers who labor incessantly to bring beauty to their classrooms in order to "heal" or to "nourish the children's senses" are so remiss in providing it for themselves. Teachers should surround themselves with beauty at home no less than at school, so that they can be refreshed and renewed at the day's end. Why not begin a veil painting on an easel in your classroom, and work on it during lunch or snacktime, so the children can watch it unfold, and experience the regeneration that you experience through form and color?

◆

It is not enough for a Waldorf teacher to search for "the inner child." *We* have to find "the inner adult" as well.

◆

Most of the Waldorf teachers that I have observed in the last two or three years are too cool to their students. Or, to put it another way, they evince the "lukewarm" quality described so negatively in the *Apocalypse of St. John*:

> *I know thy works, that thou art neither cold nor hot:*
> *I would thou wert cold or hot.*
> *So then because thou art lukewarm, and neither cold nor hot, I will spew thee out of my mouth.*

I have the impression that their coolness is a symptom of a deficit of ego-forces. It is our ego activity which generates warmth within us, which allows us to stand as warm-blooded beings who are independent of our environment; if we can draw on more ego-activity than we need to simply maintain our own warmth, then we can radiate warmth into our environment. This radiation of surplus ego-activity, this experience of sparkling enthusiasm flowing from teacher to pupil, is increasingly rare in our Waldorf classrooms. The "lack of warmth" manifested by their children's teachers is a recurrent complaint among even the most supportive Waldorf school parents.

Teachers, on their part, complain of how many problems that are beyond their control find their way into the life of the school and the classroom. Problems such as media-inspired violence, and the sexual precocity of children who have been abused, are pervasive. Is there a way, teachers ask, of protecting the soul of the school from these attacks? My belief is that by developing greater warmth, by cultivating a more outwardly-directed form of ego-activity, individual teachers (and, eventually, entire faculties) can create a protective mantle around the school; can, as it were, form something of a "School Ego." So the development of greater warmth needs to be more than a cosmetic change in a teacher's make-up; it is a step necessary to help every teacher and every school withstand the increasing attacks on the nature of the child as our century ends.

◆

Is there a "Waldorf Curriculum" written down, in black-and-white, on a piece of paper somewhere, that parents can read and *finally* understand what their child is supposed to be learning?

Well, yes—and no. The Waldorf curriculum is "written down" in the same sense that the score of Beethoven's Ninth Symphony is written down; the musical piece has little meaning until a conductor and orchestra bring it to life. No two performances of a symphony will ever be the same; no two interpretations of the "Third Grade Curriculum for the Waldorf School" will be alike; both must be brought to life again and again. Every Waldorf teacher must be at once a receptive organ and a creative instrument, re-creating Waldorf education anew, moment by moment, in her classroom.

◆

While attending a conference in Europe recently I came to realize that almost three-quarters of the German Waldorf teachers under 35 years of age were Waldorf school graduates themselves. The same proportion held true for those School of Spiritual Science Section leaders who were present at the conference. It seems likely that within fourteen years virtually all German Waldorf teachers, as well as the entire *Vorstand* of the Goetheanum, will have graduated from Waldorf schools.

And why not? Who could better serve and further the Waldorf School Movement, and the spiritual foundations from which it grew, than those individuals who were raised and nourished by both? And yet . . . A teacher trainee, describing her experiences with a distinguished Waldorf movement educator (and Waldorf school graduate) who was technically well-versed but uninspiring as a teacher, commented dryly, "But what do you expect?

He was born with an anthroposophical spoon in his mouth!" (Would that be a *copper* spoon or a *wooden* spoon?)

Is there still something to be said for those benighted souls who were not raised in anthroposophy and whose destiny it was to be denied a Waldorf education? Of what circuitous paths, torturous detours, errors in judgment and trials of soul and body do *they* have to tell us? Think of how much energy they must expend on simply trying to make some sense of the sound and fury of their life *before* they discovered anthroposophy! Having had to live in the darkness of contemporary life without anthroposophical guidance for any number of years, think of how much help they can be to those teachers who are trying to bring anthroposophy into a relationship with the modern world!

Considering the vast population of European Waldorf schools, the future prospects for the perpetuation of such "self-made anthroposophists" in Europe appear to be dismal, but still there is hope! The fragility of Waldorf education in America, the small average class size in most schools, and the difficulty of founding Waldorf high schools, all presage well for the continued existence of non-Waldorf-educated anthroposophists in the United States. Here, in the land of Self-Reliance, there are likely to be self-discovered anthroposophists and self-made Waldorf teachers, with all of their flaws and admixtures, confusion and questing—and with all that they have to give the world out of their own struggles and strivings—for many years to come.